Christian Festivals
throughout the Year

Anita Ganeri

Smart Apple Media

First published in Great Britain by Franklin Watts
96 Leonard Street, London EC2A 4XD

Franklin Watts Australia
45–51 Huntley Street, Alexandria NSW 2015
Copyright © 2003 Franklin Watts

Editor: Kate Banham, Designer: Joelle Wheelwright, Art Direction: Jonathan Hair,
Picture Research: Diana Morris, Illustrations: Peter Bull, Educational and Faith
Consultant: Alan Brown, Roman Catholic Faith Consultant: Martin Ganeri, O.P.

Published in the United States by Smart Apple Media
1980 Lookout Drive, North Mankato, MN 56003

Library of Congress Cataloging-in-Publication Data

Ganeri, Anita, 1961– Christian festivals throughout the year/ by Anita Ganeri.
p. cm. — (A year of festivals)
Summary: Introduces the main religious festivals of Christianity, telling the story behind each
festival, describing how it is celebrated around the world, and providing instructions for
related activities.
ISBN 1-58340-370-1 1. Fasts and feasts—Juvenile literature. [1. Fasts and feasts.
2. Christian life.] I. Title.
BV43.G36 2003   263'.9—dc21   2003040301

9 8 7 6 5 4 3 2 1

The publishers would like to thank the following for permission to reproduce photographs in this book:
Anthony Blake Photo Library/Photothèque Culinaire, 14b; Britstock-IFA/HAGA, 21t; Michael Dalder/
Reuters/Popperfoto, 19b; Dick Doughty/Britstock-IFA/HAGA, 13t, 25t; Bernd Ducke/Britstock-IFA,
8t, 16b; Franklin Watts Photo Libary, 6t, 16t, 23b, 26 (Steve Shott); 6b, 7t, 9t, 18b, 20t, 27t (Chris
Fairclough); 13b, 17t, 24b; Grant V. Faint/The Image Bank/Getty Images, front cover, 15; G.
Graefenhain/ Britstock-IFA, 12t; Hideo Haga/Britstock-IFA, 8b; Atsuko Isobe/Britstock-IFA/HAGA,
7c; Bruco Lucas/ Britstock-IFA, 12b; Caros Reyes-Manzo/Andes Press Agency, 14t, 17b, 20b, 22;
Akiro Nakata/ Britstock-IFA/HAGA, 23t; A. Diaz Neira/Britstock-IFA, 19t; Trip/Viesti Collection,
27b; Waldenfels/Britstock-IFA, 24t; Heidi Weidner/Britstock-IFA, 18t; Jennifer Woodcock/Reflections
Photo Library/Corbis, 10; Masakatsu Yamazaki/Britstock-IFA/HAGA, 11b.

Contents

Words printed in **bold** are explained in the glossary.

Introduction

Christians are people who follow the religion of Christianity. They believe in God and in the teachings of a man named Jesus Christ. He was a preacher and healer who lived about 2,000 years ago in the Middle East. Christians believe that Jesus was the Son of God who came to Earth to save people from their sins, or wrongdoings.

This painting shows Jesus teaching.

Spreading the word

After Jesus's death, his **disciples** spread his message far and wide. Today, with some two billion followers all over the world, Christianity is the largest religion. There are many different groups of Christians. The three largest are the Roman Catholics, Protestants, and Orthodox Christians.

Many Christian buildings are decorated with beautiful stained-glass windows like this.

Christian worship

On Sundays and other special occasions, many Christians go to church. They take part in services that include prayers, **hymns**, readings from the **Bible** (the Christian holy book), and a talk or sermon. One of the services is the sharing of bread and wine to remember the Last Supper (see page 18). This is called the **Eucharist**, Mass, or Holy Communion. Christians also pray in private to thank and praise God.

Christians worshipping in a church.

A statue of Jesus is carried through the streets in this Easter procession in Guatemala.

The Christian year

Festivals are joyful times when people remember the lives of their teachers and leaders, and events from their religion's history. These are occasions for people to celebrate and share their beliefs with special services, ceremonies, gifts, and food. Many Christian festivals mark important times in the life of Jesus. The Christian year begins with preparations for Christmas and Jesus's birth.

Festival dates

Some festivals, such as Christmas, use the everyday calendar and fall on the same date every year. Other festivals are called moveable feasts. Easter is one of these. It is based on the appearance of the springtime full moon and can change by more than a month each year. Festivals in the Orthodox Church fall on different dates because it uses an old calendar that runs several days behind.

Advent

On December 25, Christians celebrate Christmas Day and the birth of Jesus. This is one of the most important festivals in the Christian year. The period leading up to Christmas Day is called Advent, and it is the start of the Christian year. The word "Advent" means "arrival" or "coming."

In Germany, people can buy all sorts of Christmas goods at cheerful Advent markets.

An Advent service in a church in Australia.

Advent Sunday

Advent begins four Sundays before Christmas and is a time for reflecting on Jesus's birth. The first Sunday of Advent is called Advent Sunday. On this day, many Christians attend a special service in church. There are readings from the Bible and Advent hymns that look to the coming of a great savior. It is a time for looking forward with hope and expectation.

Light of the world

In some churches, Christians light candles on an Advent ring, or wreath. This is a circle of holly and ivy leaves with four small candles around the outside—one for each Sunday of Advent—and a large white one in the center. The outer candles can be red or purple, the special colors used in Christian churches at times of preparation such as Advent or Lent (see page 16). One of these outer candles is lit for each Sunday of Advent. On Christmas Day, the center candle is also lit. Christians use the candles as symbols to stand for Jesus, because he brought light and hope into the world.

◀ ⋯⋯⋯
Lighting a candle on the Advent ring.

Advent calendars

Some people mark off the days leading up to Christmas on an Advent calendar.

To make an Advent calendar:

1. Draw a Christmas scene on a large sheet of cardboard showing the story of Jesus's birth.

2. Above the scene, draw 23 small windows and one larger window. Number the small windows 1–23 and the larger one 24. Carefully cut around three sides of all the windows so they can be opened.

3. Place the window cardboard on top of a second piece of cardboard the same size. Open the windows carefully and trace inside the boxes. Then press the windows shut again.

4. On the second piece of cardboard, stick a picture in each of the boxes you have traced. You can either draw your own pictures or cut them from old Christmas cards. Then spread glue along the edge of the cardboard and place the first sheet on top facing outward.

5. Starting on December 1, open one window each day to show a Christmas picture.

The Christmas Story

Christians celebrate Jesus's birthday on December 25, but no one knows exactly when Jesus was born. Early Christians chose this date about 300 years after Jesus's birth. It was also the date of an ancient Roman winter festival, when people looked forward to spring and the return of the sun. In the Orthodox Church, Christmas falls on January 7 (see page 7).

A Christmas Carol

"O little town of Bethlehem,
How still we see thee lie!
Above thy deep and dreamless sleep
The silent stars go by.
Yet in thy dark streets shineth
The everlasting light.
The hopes and fears of all the years
Are met in thee tonight."

The Christmas story

The story of Jesus's birth is told in the books, or **Gospels**, of St. Luke and St. Matthew in the Bible. Luke tells how the angel **Gabriel** appeared to a **Jewish** woman named Mary and told her that she would have a son who would be the savior of the world. Mary and her husband, Joseph, had to travel to **Bethlehem** to pay their taxes, and there Jesus was born. Soon afterwards, shepherds tending their flocks on the nearby hills came to the stable to worship him.

At Christmas, children act out the story of Jesus's birth with nativity plays at some schools and churches.

Christmas in church

Christmas is a joyful time for Christians because it celebrates the coming of Jesus. On the night before Christmas, Christmas Eve, many churches hold a special service called Midnight Mass. On Christmas morning, people go to church to sing **carols**, listen to readings of the Christmas story from the Bible, and thank God for sending Jesus to them.

A Christingle

Some churches hold a Christingle service at Christmas to celebrate God's gifts to the world. The word "Christingle" means "Christ light."

To make a Christingle:

1. Push a small candle into the top of an orange.

2. Add four toothpicks full of nuts, raisins, and candy.

3. Tie a red ribbon around the orange.

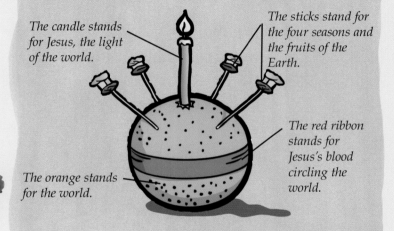

The candle stands for Jesus, the light of the world.

The sticks stand for the four seasons and the fruits of the Earth.

The orange stands for the world.

The red ribbon stands for Jesus's blood circling the world.

St. Lucia's Day

In Sweden, Christmas celebrations begin on December 13. This is St. Lucia's Day. Legend says that Saint Lucia helped the early Christians hiding from **persecution** in Rome. She is also the **patron saint** of light. On this day, girls take turns to be St. Lucia and dress in long white robes with red sashes. On their heads they wear crowns of evergreen leaves and candles to light up the winter darkness.

Girls in Sweden dress up for St. Lucia's Day.

Christmas Customs

Christmas is a happy time when Christians thank God for Jesus's birth and remember the Christmas message of peace on Earth and goodwill toward everyone. Christmas customs include putting up Christmas trees and decorations, exchanging gifts and cards, and enjoying delicious Christmas food. Today, Christmas is celebrated all over the world by Christians and non-Christians alike.

Christmas Day on the beach!

Giving gifts

Exchanging Christmas presents reminds Christians of the wise men's visit to Jesus and the gifts they brought (see page 14). Christians also give gifts to remember that Jesus was God's gift to the world. Many children leave out socks, stockings, shoes, or pillowcases, hoping they will be filled with presents. There are many stories about who delivers the Christmas gifts. In the Netherlands, children receive their presents on December 6, St. Nicholas's Day. Legend says that Saint Nicholas, or Sinterklaas (Santa Claus), was a **bishop** who lived long ago in Myra, Turkey. A story tells how he secretly left three bags of gold as gifts for three girls who were too poor to get married.

Christmas dinner is a time for families to get together to enjoy a special meal.

St. Stephen's Day

The day after Christmas is the feast of Saint Stephen, the first Christian **martyr**. He was put to death for teaching about Jesus. In Britain, it is also called Boxing Day. In the past, boxes of money, clothes, and food were opened and shared among the poor.

A delicious Christmas pudding. ....➤

Festive food

Many special types of food are eaten at Christmas. In Britain and many other places, Christmas Day dinner is traditionally roast turkey, followed by Christmas pudding and mince pies. In some countries, the main Christmas meal is eaten on Christmas Eve. In Italy, fish with lentils is a favorite Christmas dish. In Poland, people traditionally eat poppy seed cake, beet soup, and prune dumplings. An empty setting is often left at the table for the baby Jesus.

Epiphany

Twelve days after Christmas, on January 6, Christians celebrate Epiphany. St. Matthew's Gospel tells how a bright star guided the kings, or wise men, to Bethlehem, where they found Jesus. They brought three precious gifts for him, which have special meanings for Christians. There was gold fit for a king, frankincense for use in worship, and myrrh to foretell a death.

The Festival of the Three Kings in Panama. The Bible does not say how many wise men there were. It is thought there were three because they brought three gifts.

Three Kings' Day

In Spain, Epiphany is called Three Kings' Day. This is the day on which children receive their Christmas presents. On Epiphany eve, they leave their shoes by the window or door for the wise men to fill with gifts as they pass by. They also leave straw and water for the wise men's camels. If children misbehave, the wise men leave them lumps of coal instead.

Epiphany is also the end of the Twelve Days of Christmas. In many countries, a special Twelfth Night cake is baked. It often contains lucky gifts or money.

Candlemas

The festival of Candlemas falls on February 2, 40 days after Christmas. For some people, this marks the real end of Christmas. The festival gets its name from the procession of lighted candles that once took place in church. In Roman Catholic churches, there are still candlelit processions.

Jesus in the temple

On Candlemas, Christians also remember the presentation of Jesus in the **Temple** in **Jerusalem**. According to Jewish customs, Jewish boys were taken to the Temple by their parents 40 days after their birth to be "presented," or shown, to God. This was a way of thanking God for the baby's birth. At this time, Mary, Jesus's mother, was also blessed.

Candlelight is a symbol for Jesus as a guiding light in the world.

A Candlemas prayer

An old man named Simeon spoke these words when he saw Jesus in the Temple. They show that Simeon knew how special Jesus was. They are known as the *Nunc Dimittis*, which is **Latin** for "Now let us depart," and are often said as part of a church service:

"Lord, now let your servant go in peace. Your word has been fulfilled. My own eyes have seen the salvation which you have prepared in the sight of every people. A light to reveal you to the nations and the glory of your people Israel." (The Bible, Luke 2: 29–32)

Lent

For Christians, Easter is the most important festival of the year. This is when they remember how Jesus was put to death on the cross, and how he rose again from the dead. Lent is the name for the period of 40 days before Easter (not counting Sundays). This is a solemn time for Christians when they reflect on and prepare for the great festival of Easter.

*Jesus was put to death by being **crucified**, or nailed to a cross. Many churches have models or statues commemorating this. The models are called crucifixes.*

Carnival time is particularly colorful in Rio de Janeiro, Brazil.

Carnival!

Lent begins in February or March. The day before Lent is called Shrove Tuesday. In many countries, particularly in South America, Shrove Tuesday, or Mardi Gras, is carnival time! Spectacular processions of floats, singers, and dancers fill the streets with color and noise. This is a time for partying before the solemn days of Lent begin. The word *Shrove* comes from an old word that means "to confess your sins." Some Christians go to church to ask God to forgive them for their wrongdoings.

Fasting

During Lent, Christians try to live good lives and think about Jesus's suffering. Before he began his teaching, Jesus spent 40 days in the wilderness. There he was tempted by the Devil, who tried to turn him away from God. Lent used to be a time for **fasting**, or going without food, as Jesus did in the wilderness. Today, many people still give up luxuries such as sweets. They may also give money to charity and spend more time reading the Bible.

Pancake Day

Because Christians traditionally ate plain, simple food during Lent, on Shrove Tuesday they had to use up their rich foods, such as fat, eggs, and milk, which would go bad if kept. In Britain, these were made into delicious pancakes, and Shrove Tuesday is often called Pancake Day.

Ash Wednesday

The first day of Lent is called Ash Wednesday. In Roman Catholic churches, a special mass is said. Last year's palm branches (see page 18) are burned and the ashes mixed with holy water. Then the priest makes a cross shape with the ash on each person's forehead. Lent is a time for thinking of the things you have done wrong, and ashes are a sign of being sorry.

Mother's Day

For some Christians, Mothering Sunday, or Mother's Day, falls on the fourth Sunday of Lent. In church, special prayers are said for mothers to thank them for all their hard work. Children often give their mothers gifts of cards and flowers.

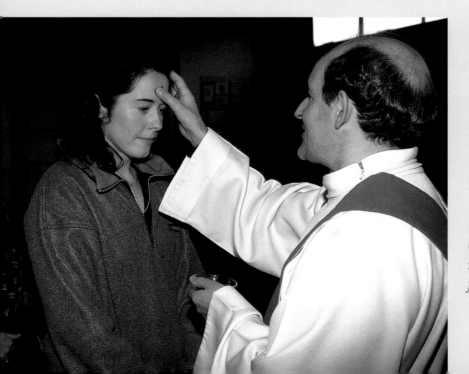

On Ash Wednesday, the priest makes an ash mark on the forehead of each worshipper.

Holy Week

The last week of Lent is called Holy Week. It is the most important time in the Christian year, when Christians remember the final week of Jesus's life. There are many special church services, prayers, and processions.

Palm Sunday

Holy Week begins with Palm Sunday, when Jesus rode into Jerusalem on the back of a donkey for the festival of **Passover** (Pesach). Crowds of people greeted him as a great king and savior. They waved palm branches to welcome him. Today, people who go to church are given small palm-leaf crosses or even palm branches to remind them of that day.

On Palm Sunday in Germany, people are given willow twigs instead of palm crosses or branches.

The Last Supper

On Thursday of Holy Week, Jesus ate a final meal with his 12 disciples. This is called the Last Supper. At the meal, he took some bread and wine and shared them with the disciples. He told them that the bread and wine represented his body and his blood, which he was about to sacrifice for the sins of mankind. Today, most Christians receive bread and wine as part of a special church service to remember Jesus. This service has different names, such as Mass, Holy Communion, or the Eucharist, and happens regularly throughout the year, not just during Holy Week.

The minister or priest blesses the bread and wine that is used in Holy Communion.

Maundy Thursday

This Thursday is called Maundy, or Holy, Thursday. *Maundy* comes from the Latin word *mandatum*, which means "a command." On this day, Jesus gave his disciples the commands to share bread and wine, and to love one another. He showed his love for them by washing their feet, as a humble servant would. In some churches, the priest washes the feet of 12 worshippers.

The Semana Santa, or Holy Week, procession in Seville, Spain. Some people dress in hoods and robes as a sign of sorrow. ·······························➤

Good Friday

On Friday of Holy Week, Christians remember how Jesus was crucified. It is called Good Friday because Christians believe that Jesus gave up his life for the good of everyone. This is a solemn day when most churches are cleared of their flowers and decorations and left dark and plain with a simple cross on the **altar**. There is often a service of silent prayer between midday and three o'clock, the time that Jesus hung on the cross. On Good Friday, some people eat hot cross buns. The cross on the top reminds them of how Jesus died.

◄··········
Every 10 years in Oberammergau, Germany, the story of Holy Week is acted out on a grand scale.

19

Easter Sunday

After the sadness of Good Friday, Easter Sunday is a joyful day. This is the day on which Christians believe Jesus was resurrected, or rose from the dead. Christians believe that this shows that death is not the end, but the start of a new life with God. Many Christians go to church to thank God for Jesus's life. Churches are filled with beautiful flowers, and the church bells ring out.

On Easter Day

When Jesus died, his friends took his body down from the cross and placed it in a tomb. They rolled a large stone across the entrance. Three days later, on Sunday morning, they went to visit the tomb. To their astonishment, the tomb was empty. Jesus had risen from the dead.

Easter Vigil

The Easter **Vigil** is the most important service of the year for Roman Catholics. After dark on Easter eve, a fire is lit outside or inside the church. The Paschal, or Easter, candle is lit from the fire. Then everyone lights a candle from the Easter candle. They proceed into the church as an ancient hymn called the *Exultet*, which means "rejoice," is sung (see opposite). A similar service is held in Orthodox churches.

Lighting the Paschal, or Easter, candle at an Easter Vigil in South Africa.

Easter customs

Easter customs, such as decorating Easter eggs, celebrate new life. They remind Christians of how Jesus rose from the dead. But they also celebrate spring and a time of new life in nature.

The Easter egg rolling competition happens every year on the lawn of the White House in Washington, D.C., the home of the U.S. president.

Decorated Easter eggs

In some countries, such as the U.S., people decorate their own Easter eggs.

To decorate an Easter egg:

1. Use a needle to make a tiny hole in each end of an egg. Gently blow through one hole so that the egg comes out of the other. (You could use a hard-boiled egg instead.)

2. Draw a pattern on the empty shell with a color crayon.

3. Dip the egg in a bowl of dye or food coloring. It will stain the shell except where the pattern appears.

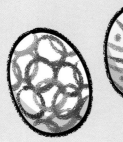

The Exultet

"Rejoice, heavenly powers!
Sing, choirs of angels!
Exult, all creation around God's throne!
Jesus Christ, our King, is risen!
Sound the trumpet of salvation!"

Summer Festivals

Ascension Day

Forty days after Easter, Christians remember the end of Jesus's time on Earth after his resurrection and his going into heaven to be with God forever. This is called Ascension Day and always falls on a Thursday. ("Ascension" means "to go up.")

Pentecost is a popular time for people to be **baptized** *and join the Christian Church. Traditionally, they dress in white to signify the start of a new life.*

Pentecost

The festival of Pentecost, 50 days after Easter, marks the birthday of the Christian Church. The Bible tells how, at Pentecost, a strong wind blew through the house where Jesus's disciples were praying in Jerusalem, and flames rested on their heads. They were filled with the Holy Spirit and began to speak in many different languages about God's work. This is when they began to go out and teach people about Jesus. Christians believe that the Holy Spirit is always with them, helping and guiding them.

Trinity Sunday

The Sunday after Pentecost is called Trinity Sunday. On this day, Christians think about the three ways of seeing God — God the Father, who made and cares for the world; God the Son, who came to Earth as Jesus; and God the Holy Spirit, the power of God. Saint Patrick, the patron saint of Ireland, explained that the three parts of God were like the three parts of a shamrock leaf — separate but part of the same whole.

Corpus Christi

The Thursday after Trinity Sunday is the Roman Catholic festival of *Corpus Christi*, meaning "the body of Christ." The festival was begun in 1264 and celebrates the Last Supper. The bread used for Holy Communion may be carried through the streets as part of a procession. Often the path of the procession is scattered with flowers. Some people kneel as the procession passes to honor the bread, which is a symbol of Jesus Christ. In the Middle Ages, this was also a time when **mystery plays** were performed.

During the Corpus Christi procession in Italy, the bread is carried through the town under a canopy.

The Assumption

For Roman Catholics and Orthodox Christians, the Blessed Virgin Mary, Jesus's mother, is a very special person whom they honor and worship. On August 15, they remember how Mary, at the end of her life, was taken up into heaven. Roman Catholics call this the Feast of the Assumption of Our Lady. (Here "assumed" means "taken up.") It is a holiday in many Roman Catholic countries. In the Orthodox Church, it is called the Dormition, or Falling Asleep, of the Blessed Virgin Mary.

A painting of the Blessed Virgin Mary, Jesus's mother.

Harvest Festival

In September or October, many Christians in Britain go to special services to celebrate Harvest Festival. This is a time for thanking God for all the good things that come from the earth. Churches are decorated with flowers, fruit, vegetables, and loaves of harvest bread. These are later given to charity to share God's goodness. In other countries, the harvest is celebrated at different times of the year.

A colorful display of fruit and vegetables in church for Harvest Festival.

Harvest bread is often baked in the shape of a wheat sheaf.

Harvest supper

For farmers, autumn was traditionally the time for bringing in the crops. When the last stalks of grain had been cut, a great feast was held to thank God for the harvest. Some churches still hold a harvest supper. Long ago, a loaf was baked from wheat cut at the start of the harvest. The bread was used at a Holy Communion service on August 1. This became Lammas, or Loaf Mass, Day.

Thanksgiving

On the fourth Thursday in November, people in the U.S. celebrate the first harvest of the early settlers in America almost 400 years ago. Life was hard, so when the harvest was safely gathered in, the settlers gave heartfelt thanks to God. Many families dress up in their best clothes and go to church. Then they share a delicious Thanksgiving dinner of turkey and pumpkin pie. Thanksgiving is a very important festival and a national holiday.

A family enjoying a delicious Thanksgiving dinner in the U.S.

A harvest altar cloth

A church's altar is covered by an altar cloth. The design of the cloth changes to reflect the church's year. At festival times, it is usually white or gold, with an appropriate design.

To make a harvest altar cloth:

1. Cut a piece of white or gold cloth about 80 inches (203 cm) long by 20 inches (50 cm) wide. Turn over the edges and pin the hems down.

2. Cut out the shapes of a cross, loaves of bread, sheaves of corn, fruit, and vegetables from colored cloth. Sew or pin them onto your altar cloth.

A Harvest Hymn

"We plow the fields,
and scatter
The good seed on the land,
But it is fed and watered
By God's almighty hand.
He sends the snow in winter,
The warmth to swell the grain,
The breezes and the sunshine,
And soft refreshing rain.
All good gifts around us
Are sent from heaven above.
Then thank the Lord,
O thank the Lord,
For all his love."

All Saints' and All Souls'

On November 1, some Christians celebrate All Saints' Day, when they give thanks for the life and works of all the saints. For all Christians, saints are especially holy people who devoted their lives to God. Roman Catholics and Orthodox Christians pray to the saints for help and guidance. Apart from All Saints' Day, each of the saints has a special day throughout the year on which he or she is remembered. This is called a feast day. In the Roman Catholic Church, feast days are important festivals.

Saint Peter

Saint Peter was one of Jesus's disciples who became the leader of the Christian Church. Tradition says that Peter traveled to Rome, where he became the first bishop. The leader of the Roman Catholic Church, the Pope, is also called the Bishop of Rome. St. Peter was crucified for his beliefs. His feast day is on June 29, and he shares it with Saint Paul.

Saints are an important focus of worship in the Orthodox Church. Orthodox Christians celebrate All Saints' Day earlier in the year, in June.

All Souls' Day

The day after All Saints' Day is called All Souls' Day. This is when Christians remember those who have died and pray that their souls may rest in peace in heaven. Some people visit the graves of loved ones and put flowers on them. Even so, this is not a gloomy day, but a day for happy memories.

In many countries, people place flowers on the graves of their loved ones on All Souls' Day.

Day of the Dead

In Mexico, All Souls' Day is called the Day of the Dead. People used to believe that this was a day when the souls of the dead came back to life for just one night. At home and in cemeteries, people leave out flowers, water, and food to welcome the souls of the dead. Among the offerings are models of skulls, skeletons, and coffins, made from sugar.

Sugar model-making in Mexico dates back more than 100 years. The hollow models are formed from hard white sugar and decorated with bright colors.

27

Festival Calendar

Date	Month	Event
	November/December	Advent Sunday
6	December	St. Nicholas's Day
13	December	St. Lucia's Day
25	December	Christmas Day
26	December	St. Stephen's Day
6	January	Epiphany
7	January	Christmas Day (Orthodox)
2	February	Candlemas
	February/March	Shrove Tuesday
	February/March	Lent
	March/April	Mother's Day
	March/April	Holy Week
		• Palm Sunday
		• Maundy, or Holy, Thursday
		• Good Friday
		• Holy Saturday
		• Easter Day (Sunday)
	April/May	Ascension Day
	May/June	Pentecost/Whitsun
	May/June	Trinity Sunday
	May/June	Corpus Christi
29	June	Feast of St. Peter and St. Paul
15	August	Feast of the Assumption/ Dormition (Orthodox)
	September/October	Harvest Festival
1	November	All Saints' Day
2	November	All Souls' Day
	November	Thanksgiving Day (U.S.)

Glossary

Altar	A large table in a Christian church used for the Eucharist.
Baptized	Sprinkled with, or bathed in, water to wash away sins as part of a ceremony at which a person becomes a full member of the Christian Church.
Bethlehem	A town in Israel where Jesus was born.
Bible	The holy book of the Christians. It is made up of the Old Testament and the New Testament. The Old Testament dates back to Jewish times, before the birth of Jesus; the New Testament contains the life and words of Jesus Christ.
Bishop	A leading priest responsible for all Church affairs in a particular area.
Carols	Songs usually sung at Christmas.
Crucified	Put to death by being nailed to a cross.
Disciples	The 12 men chosen by Jesus to be his close companions and followers.
Eucharist	The service at which bread and wine are shared in remembrance of Jesus. It is also called Mass or Holy Communion.
Fasting	Going without food.
Gabriel	The angel who appeared to Mary and told her that she would be the mother of Jesus.
Gospels	The first four books of the New Testament. They tell of the life and work of Jesus. The word "gospel" comes from an old word meaning "good news," because the Gospels contain the good news about Jesus.
Hymns	Religious songs that praise God.
Jerusalem	A city in Israel where Jesus spent his last days on Earth and where he was crucified.
Jewish	Relating to the faith of Judaism. Jesus's family was Jewish, and he was born and raised as a Jew.
Martyr	Someone who suffers and even dies for his or her religious beliefs.
Mystery plays	Medieval religious plays presenting Bible stories or the miracles of the saints. They are still performed today in many cities, such as York and Coventry in Britain and Oberammergau in Germany. They are also known as "miracle plays."
Passover (Pesach)	A Jewish festival celebrated in March or April. It remembers the escape of the early Jews from slavery in Egypt.
Patron saint	A saint regarded as the protector or supporter of a particular group or country. For example, Saint Christopher is the patron saint of travelers, and Saint Patrick is the patron saint of Ireland.
Persecution	The injuring or harassing of someone, usually because of what he or she believes in.
Temple	The ancient Jewish Temple in Jerusalem. It was the holiest building for the Jews.
Vigil	A time of staying awake when you would normally be asleep, as part of worship during a festival.

Further Resources

Books

Chambers, Catherine.
A World of Festivals: Christmas.
London: Evans Brothers, 1997.

Chambers, Catherine.
A World of Festivals: Easter.
London, Evans Brothers, 1998.

Koch, Carl.
The Catholic Church: Journey, Wisdom, & Mission.
Winona, Minn.: St. Mary's Press, 1994.

Senger, Mary Cay.
The Eucharist: Giving Thanks and Praise.
Collegeville, Minn.: Liturgical Press, 2000.

Watson, Carol.
Beliefs and Cultures: Christian.
London: Franklin Watts, 1996.

Web Sites

http://www.antiochian-orthodox.co.uk
Information about festivals in the Orthodox Church.

http://www.christmas.com
Christmas greetings from around the world.

http://www.festivals.com
Information about festivals, holy days, and holidays.

Index

263
GAN

Ganeri, Anita
Christian festivals
throughout the year

$16.95